Yes, in a poor man's garden grow
Far more than herbs and flowers;
Kind thoughts, contentment, peace of mind,
And joy for weary hours.

Mary Howitt 1799-1888
The Poor Man's Garden

RECIPES
for
GARDENERS

**Introduction by
Doug Goodyer**

Copper Beech Publishing

Published in Great Britain by
Copper Beech Publishing Ltd
© Copper Beech Publishing Ltd 1998

Introduction by Doug Goodyer
Editor Jan Barnes

ISBN 1 898617 23 6

A CIP catalogue record for this book is available from the
British Library.

Copper Beech Publishing Ltd
P O Box 159 East Grinstead
Sussex England RH19 4FS

Doug Goodyer is an 11th generation gardener; one of his ancestors was gardener to King Charles I. Doug is Head Gardener at Hever Castle in Kent and appears on radio and television in the UK and the United States. His speciality is Victorian and Edwardian gardening.

INTRODUCTION

Ever since man stepped out of a cave and moved on to the land, gardening has caught the imagination of people of all ages.

The greatest gardening era was the Victorian period when plant hunters went to the four corners of the earth searching for new plants for many reasons, some medical, some for food and others just to adorn our parks, pleasure gardens and later our own home gardens.

After the Victorians, the Edwardians were like children in a sweet shop with so many plants to choose from. But the legacy that spilled over right up to the present day is how best to control and manage the pests and plant diseases in our gardens.

This book is a collection of ways which our ancestors found of tackling problems in their gardens.

I remember, when I started my career as a garden boy, some of these old ways were still being used. For example, one of the recipes describes how to make liquid manure for vines, peaches and other fruit trees; one part cow dung four parts water, stir well and apply as liquid feed. A variation I remember using was to put the cow dung in a hessian sack, sink it in the water butt and use it that way.

I hope, like me, you will spend many a happy hour reading this book and perhaps try some of the recipes which will still work today.

Good Gardening.

Doug Goodyer

Apples or Pears

To preserve apples and pears, first allow the fruit to lie on the shelves in the fruit-room and sweat. Wipe dry and pack in boxes with enough dry sawdust to exclude the air from them. Sawdust from resinous woods should not be used.

Fruit packed in dry sand would keep equally well; but it is difficult to clean them from sand and the fruit will always eat gritty when so kept.

Another method …

Gather the fruit during a dry day and put it at once into earthen glazed pans. Each pan should be deep enough to contain two or three layers of fruit and have a tightly-fitting lid. If the fruit sweats, the exudation dries on the fruit's surface and helps to keep in the flavour. The cover helps to exclude the light. Keep the pans in a dry cool place and *never* wipe the fruit until required for dessert.

Asparagus

Salt and seaweed are useful for asparagus. In spring, a dressing of salt should be given to the asparagus bed, sufficient to impart a whitish surface. Seaweed when available also makes an ideal dressing.

In the autumn, the bed should be made up with leaves and manure.

Asparagus should never be cut after
Midsummer Day.

Bees

To feed, take two pounds of loaf sugar and half a pint of liquid (consisting of one quarter best vinegar, and three quarters water).

Boil together until it assumes a yellow colour, then pour into a well-greased dish and cut up before cold into strips convenient for insertion into the hives. Should it candy on cooling, it is a proof that it has not been boiled enough and should be returned to the saucepan without water and boiled again.

Bee Sting

Cure a bee sting in the following manner. Immediately after taking out the sting, get an onion, bruise it and apply it to the stung place; this will afford immediate relief. A washerwoman's blue bag applied in the same manner will have a like effect.

Black Boards

To make black boards, boil one pound of logwood in water enough to cover it and add half an ounce of green vitriol. This is superior to paint as it stains the wood and will not wear off. It dries in a few minutes, and bears no gloss.

Broccoli

To prevent club in Broccoli, mix one gallon of fresh soot and one pound of saltpetre with water to the consistency of good thick paint and dip the roots of every plant in the mixture before planting. If the ground is hot and gravelly, a good dressing of marl will be useful. The soil ought to be deepened in every way possible.

Bulbs - To pack

Let the bulbs be quite ripe, pack them in perfectly dry river (not sea) sand in a box. Case this with another, filling the space between the two, which should be two or three inches wide, with perfectly dry sawdust.

Cabbage

In old soils, all the cabbage kind and cauliflowers especially, have a tendency to form club-roots. This is due to the attacks of the larvae of the weevil.

When planting, it is advisable to make a thick puddle of lime and soot and dip the root and stem of each young plant in it, in order to render them distasteful to the maggot.

Charcoal dust, spread half an inch thick on the plot, and then just mixed in by the point of the spade, will sometimes act as a preventive.

A dressing of lime from the gas-works, at the rate of twelve bushels to the acre, is also effectual.

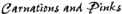

Carnations and Pinks

Beds of carnations and pinks may be protected from rabbits by simply adding a few Congreve matches around the plants; the smell is very offensive to rabbits and they will not come near them.

Carrots and Onions

This is a recipe for the very best carrots and onions. Before growing carrots and onions, dress the ground with lime, soot and a small quantity of salt.

Celery

Spray celery with a mixture of soft soap, water and paraffin to prevent celery maggot.

Cherry Trees

Blackfly on cherry trees is best destroyed by tobacco-water. The most economical way of applying it is by dipping the affected leaves into a basin containing the tobacco-water.

Cucumber and Melon Seed

When the fruit is first cut, the seed should be put into a bowl of water; that which swims on the surface is worthless; the good will sink to the bottom. This can only be depended upon at the time the fruit is first cut; if the seed has been dried and kept for any length of time, it will probably all swim, though it has not lost its vegetating properties.

Cucumbers - To keep quite fresh

When cucumbers are at their best they should be cut and laid in a box made for the purpose. Then bury the box in some dry sand, covering it over to the depth of a foot. If laid in the box in this way, their colour and bloom may be preserved for a fortnight and they will look as fresh as the day they were cut.

There should not be any hay or moss put with the cucumbers in the box, as this will cause them to turn yellow.

Cut Flowers

To preserve cut flowers for the greatest length of time, their stems should be put in a glass of water and the glass put to stand on a plate. Place a bell-glass over it with the edges previously wetted, so that when it comes into contact with the plate it may prevent the air passing between, thus securing them as air-tight as possible. The flowers will keep fresh a long time.

If some charcoal has been previously steeped in the water, or a small piece of camphor dissolved, it will greatly assist in keeping the flowers fresh. Violets may be preserved for a long time by sticking them with short stems into a glass dish filled with damp silver sand and then inverting a tumbler over them.

Dahlias

Dahlia roots can be preserved through the winter. Firstly, dig up the roots as soon as the first frost has spoiled their foliage.

Cut the stems off about six inches above the tubers, then lay them in a greenhouse to dry. Once dry, pack them in dry sand and keep in a cellar. They must remain there till they begin to grow in spring, when they may be taken and planted in the borders.

Damping or Fogging off

Cuttings in heat and seedlings pricked out are very liable to damp off if left in confined air with too much moisture.

The best mode of treatment is, as soon as damping appears, to give more air and increase the temperature five degrees. At the same time, sprinkle the surface of the soil with a mixture of silver sand and powdered peat, crumbled to the fineness of snuff.

Docks and Dandelions

The most simple and effectual way to kill docks and dandelions is to cut the tops off in the spring or summer time and pour some gas-tar, or sprinkle some salt, on the wound.

Either of these will kill the root, by eating to the very extremity.

Filberts

If you wish to preserve with their husks on, let them remain on the trees till the husks turn yellow, then gather them (when dry) and spread them out on a table or floor in a warm dry place. They should not be exposed to much light, air or draught.

Examine them every two or three days to see that neither damp nor mould attacks them. If it does, they must be removed to a still drier place until the husks have become brown and all the moisture has evaporated. Then put them in jars and keep them in a dry room till wanted.

Filberts will keep in this way for twelve months and look as fresh as when they were first gathered.

Fish Ponds

When there is no stone base, the bottom of a pond should be puddled with clay and then covered with coarse gravel. The clay should be from six to twelve inches thick, well worked with water into a tenacious paste and then beaten or trodden with the naked feet into a close mass.

Instead of a regular slope, it is best to form the sides in the manner of terraces, so that the flower-pots containing aquatic plants may be dropped into their places on a series of descending shelves and removed again for the winter, if the plants require protection. Where plants such as lilies are to remain permanently, strong loam should be laid on the clay for them, and the whole covered with gravel before letting the water in.

Flowers in a Garden

It is recommended that blue flowers be placed next to orange, and violet next to yellow; whilst red and pink flowers are never to be seen to greater advantage than when surrounded by verdure and by white flowers. The latter may also be advantageously dispersed among groups of blue and orange, and violet and yellow flowers.

Plants whose flowers are to produce a contrast should be of the same size; and in many cases the colour of the sand or gravel-walks, or beds of a garden, should be made to conduce to the general effect.

Fruit Trees - To cure gumming

The place where the gum accumulates should be well washed and cleaned and then stopped well up with a paste made of horse-dung, clay and tar. This will prevent the accumulation of the gum, and will assist the wound in healing over.

Fruit Trees - To remove scale

Take one quart sweet oil, one quart spirits of ammonia and one third of a pint spirits of turpentine.

Mix these liquids together and wash fruit trees with a brush in the winter-time. Take care not to touch the buds. Train oil or any fish oil applied in the same manner, will prove equally satisfactory in destroying the scale.

Fungi - To dry for a Herbarium

Some of the dry firm kinds of fungi may be wrapped up carefully in clean blotting-paper, and laid near the fire.

Another method is to have ready a number of tin boxes, partially filled with dry silver sand. The specimens should be dropped into the sand with their gills upwards and quite covered with sand sprinkled finely into every crevice. The sand will prevent them from shrinking. When the boxes are filled, a gentle tap will shake the sand still closer.

These boxes are to be placed without lids, in a rather cool oven or on a shelf near the fire, so as to dry quickly. If the heat is too great, the fungi will be apt to lose colour. In a week they will be quite dry and the sand may be shaken out. They can then be mounted in a cabinet and they will preserve their shape and much of their original colour for years.

Gardener's Boots - To waterproof

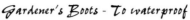

Melt and mix well the following over a fire: one pint of boiled linseed oil, half a pound of mutton suet, six ounces of clean beeswax and four ounces of resin.

While warm, but not hot enough to shrink the leather, with a brush lay on plentifully over new boots and shoes. The leather remains pliant.

The New England fishermen preserve their boots watertight by this method, which, it is said, has been in use among them above one hundred years! The boots can thus stand in water hour after hour without inconvenience.

Greenfly
To prevent greenfly on apple trees

One pound of sulphur vivum
One pound Scotch snuff
One pound quicklime
Half pound lampblack
One pound soft soap

Mix together with water sufficient to make it into the consistency of paint. Unnail your trees about February before the bloom-buds begin to swell and, with a common paint-brush, paint every branch from the ground upwards.

The application must be made every other, if not every year; but once in two years may be sufficient.

Greenfly

To remove greenfly from house, pit or frame, choose a still evening and let your plants be quite dry. Place them close together and in a close space thus obtained, put either an iron pan or hard-burnt garden pot.

Add a few red-hot cinders that do not smoke, upon which put your tobacco or tobacco-paper; a cloud of smoke will soon arise.

When the frame is well filled with smoke, remove the pan, but be exceedingly careful that the tobacco does not break out into a flame.

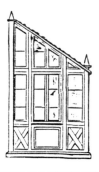

Herbarium - to dry plants

Specimens should be gathered when quite dry and spread out between two sheets of thick blotting paper. Great care should be taken in spreading out the leaves and petals so as to display the structure of the plant.

Place the paper in a warm room under slight pressure, just enough to keep the specimen in position, but not enough to crush the leaves or bruise the petals of the flower; the paper should be changed every 24 hours. Continue this till the specimens are completely dry.

Heaths are sometimes difficult to dry to preserve their foliage; when first cut, the specimens should be dipped in scalding water and then laid to dry in the usual way. They will seldom lose their foliage if treated in this way; it will also take the gumminess off the flowers, and greatly facilitate their drying.

Herbs - To dry

The best state in which mint, balm, thyme, sage and other kitchen or medicinal herbs can be gathered for drying and preserving for winter use, is just as their flowers are opening. At that period of growth they are found to contain more of the essential oil, on which their flowers depend, than at any other.

Hydrangeas - how to make the flower blue

If the Hydrangea is grown in a strong maiden loam, which contains a portion of oxide of iron, the flower will come blue without further trouble. However, they will require to be potted in this compost and continually grown in the same.

If the soil itself will not produce the flower blue, they should be watered with a solution of alum for some time previous to flowering. The solution may be made by mixing at the rate of one ounce of alum to a gallon of rain water.

For cuttings, the plants should be struck from small cuttings of the soft wood, from February till May.

Old plants cannot be depended upon to produce blue flowers.

Ice - To preserve

The chief requisite to preserve ice is to pound it very small, beat it firmly together and exclude the air from it by means of a good covering of straw. Where there is an ice-well for the purpose, the ice should be well pounded with wooden mallets and then deposited in the ice-well. Ram it down well, keeping a tier of straw between the ice and the wall. This will keep the ice from wasting. The ice-well should be well drained, but the drain should be so constructed as not to admit air to the bottom of the well, or the bulk of ice will be greatly diminished by it.

Ice-wells are the best places to keep ice for any length of time, but another method is to make a large heap of finely-powdered ice on the top of a dry bank and cover with straw of fern to the thickness of two or three feet. If it is beaten firmly together into a heap, it will keep a supply for the following summer.

Labels for Plants

Cut some pieces of zinc to the size required and with a quill pen write the names of the plants in nitro-muriate of platinum. This will become perfectly black and remain legible for many years.

Another method

Cut pieces of zinc as above and paint them white. When dry, write the names with a black-lead pencil in a good round hand, then varnish. This is a more elegant way and is not affected by weather.

Lettuce and Strawberry-beds
To protect from snails

If the beds are surrounded by a slate or board-edging, made to stand 5 inches above the ground, and occasionally coated with a paste made of train oil and soot, it will form a barrier over which snails will not pass.

Liquid Manures

For vines, peaches, standard apple, and other fruit trees, measure by weight one part of cow-dung, with four parts of tepid water, (or the collected drainage of the cow-house or pig-sty, diluted with a similar quantity of water).

Most flowering shrubs relish a liquid manure made of soot, in the proportion of six quarts of soot to a hogshead of water.

Marble
To clean

Two parts common soda
One part pumice stone
One part finely powdered chalk
Water

Sift the soda, pumice stone and chalk through a fine sieve and mix it with water. Rub the solution well over the marble and the stains will be removed. Afterwards, wash the marble over with soap and water and it will be as clean as it was originally.

Melons
Melons and gourds do not succeed in poor soils, especially if of a sandy nature.

Where rich loam is scarce, the scrapings of ponds and ditches will make a good substitute.

Mistletoe

To grow mistletoe on apple trees use the following method. In the month of March, make two cuts, in the shape of the letter V, on the under side of a branch of an apple-tree. The incisions must be made quite down to the wood of the tree. Raise the tongue of the bark (but not enough to break it), and put underneath one or two seeds, freshly squeezed from ripe mistletoe berries.

Seedlings soon appear, and remain attached to the branch; their growth seems to cause no injury to the tree.

Moles - To extirpate

Take some green leaves of the common elder, and strew them in the subterranean paths of the mole. The smell of these leaves is very offensive to the mole and will soon cause this little creature to disappear.

Moss - on Fruit Trees

Every second year fruit trees should be well scrubbed with a scrubbing brush dipped in strong brine. Be sure to moisten every part of the bark of the stem and branches. This not only destroys the moss but insects of all kinds and is beneficial to all trees, whereas applications of lime choke up the respiratory pores and sometimes produce canker.

Moss on Gravel Walks

Moss may be kept down by the use of a broom made of wire. If the wire bristles are made of iron the broom should be well dried and dipped in oil before and after being used.

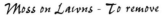

Moss on Lawns - To remove

Water the lawn with a weak solution of ammoniacal liquor; one gallon of this liquor is sufficient to mix with four gallons of water. This should be put on with a rose waterpot. The grass will look brown afterwards for a while, but it will soon redeem its verdure.

Another method

Procure some very fine siftings of coal-ashes and sow them all over the parts where moss abounds. The presence of moss indicates that the soil is exhausted, and a top-dressing of nitrate of soda or soot will be found beneficial.

If the grass is made to thrive, it will always choke the moss.

Names on Fruit

To grow names on wall fruit, cut some small pieces of paper in the shape of letters and paste them on peaches and nectarines with gum. Do this just before they begin to turn colour. They should always be pasted on the side that is most exposed to the sun. When the fruit is ripe, the paper should be taken off, and it will leave the exact print on the fruit.

Onions
Grub in onions

Make some strong lime-water, and add enough soot to make it into a thin paint. With this, water the crop the moment the maggot appears. This soot mixture should always be used to increase the weight of the crop.

Another method

House-slops mixed with lime and soot both destroy the maggot and improve the plant; but unless rain follows immediately, it is advisable to drench the ground with pure water the day after application.

Orchids

To kill scale on orchids mix together half pound of camphor, one pint spirits of wine, one pound Scotch snuff, one pound ground black pepper and one pound flowers of sulphur.

Put the mixture in a bottle carefully stopped and sprinkle it on the infested orchid plants occasionally.

Parsley - To dry for Winter Use

Pull or cut your parsley when full grown and hang it in the sun to dry, taking care not to allow it to get wet. It may afterwards be tied in bunches and hung up in a dry room till wanted. When required, a little should be rubbed in the palm of the hand and put in the pot; it will immediately resume its colour, flavour and smell, even though it has been kept for years.

Pathways

A cheap asphalt for walks is easy to make. The area must first be previously levelled, then put on it a coat of tar and sift some road-sand or coal-ashes all over it very thickly. After this is dry repeat the operation until you have got four coats of tar, and as many of coal-ashes or road-sand. You will then have an excellent clean, dry and hard path. It will make excellent walks, or floors for sheds, out-buildings, etc., and will wear for many years.

Peaches

Cotton wool can protect peaches from wasps. Draw a little cotton wool very thin and fasten it round the fruit. This will protect the peaches from wasps and will not affect the flavour or colour of the fruit, providing it is not put on too long before the fruit begins to ripen.

Peach and Nectarine Trees

Peach trees and nectarines are often attacked with greenfly and may be fumigated on the open walls in the following manner:

Procure two poles long enough to reach from the top of the wall to the bottom and stand them one at each side of the tree. Allow them to rest against the top of the wall, and stand them two feet away at the bottom. Then get a carpet or blanket and lay it over them, securing it well to the wall on each side, so that it will not allow the smoke to escape. The smoke may be blown underneath the bottom by means of a fumigating pipe, or a No. 24 pot may be half filled with red-hot coals, and put to stand under the carpet, and some tobacco shaked lightly on the top.

The day after the tree has been fumigated, it should be well washed with the engine or syringe, and the ground digged underneath.

Peas

This is to protect peas from slugs and snails. Lay a train of slaked lime or wood-ashes on each side of the row of peas and the snails will not pass over it.

To keep Mice and Sparrows from Peas

Sow soot with the peas, to keep the sparrows from nibbling the young tops as soon as the peas come through the ground. Dress the rows with soot when the plants are damp. Soot is one of the richest of manures, so the crop will benefit by its use.

To protect peas from mice, strew sawdust half an inch thick, over the soil after the peas are sown and raked. Mice never touch it and birds will never meddle with the peas when they appear through it.

Plant sticks

To prevent the bottoms of plant-sticks rotting, dip the bottoms of the plant-sticks into hot asphalt three or four times, until the asphalt is the sixteenth of an inch thickness on them. This will preserve them a long time.

Those that have not the convenience of dipping them in asphalt, may dip them in tar until it adheres to them to the above thickness.

Ponds

To clear duckweed off ponds

A few ducks turned on to a pond where this unsightly weed abounds will usually devour it.

Another method

Twist a straw or hay-band long enough to reach from one side of the pond to the other. Then two men should take hold one at each end and drag it gently from one end to the other. The band will swim on the top, and take all the duckweed before it.

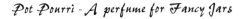

Pot Pourri - A perfume for Fancy Jars

Half a pound of common salt, quarter of a pound of saltpetre, quarter of an ounce of stroax, six cloves, one handful of dried bay leaves and one handful of dried lavender flowers form the basis of the Pot Pourri.

This will last for years, and you may add to it annually petals of roses and of other fragrant flowers gathered on dry days, as fancy may dictate. By the same rule you may add powdered benzoin, chips of sandalwood, cinnamon, orris root and musk.

A very excellent Pot Pourri may be made in winter with: one pound of dried rose petals (bought at a chemist) four ounces of salt, two ounces of saltpetre, eight drops of essence of ambergris, six drops of essence of lemon, four drops of oil of cloves, four drops of oil of lavender and two drops of essence of bergamot.

Rabbits

Prevent hares and rabbits barking trees with this wash.

Take one part tar, one part lime and two parts cow-dung. Mix together and apply it to the stems of the trees by means of a brush. Where appearance is not an object, lime-wash alone may be applied and would prove equally efficient.

Rape-dust, as a Manure

The seeds of the rape plant, after the oil has been extracted from it, are a fertilizer of great value. Eight tons of rape-dust afford as much nitrogen as one hundred tons of farm-yard manure. It has been proved that rape-dust possesses the power of absorbing from twice to ten times as much atmospheric moisture as the finest soils.

Roses - To destroy Maggot in

A bushel of unslaked lime in powder, half a pound of sulphur also in powder, water and soot should be used as follows.

Mix the lime and sulphur well whilst dry, then add water and boil for one hour. After that add soot moistened to the same consistency, just enough to darken the colour. In the latter part of February, brush the mixture all over the rose plants.

Roses and Pelargoniums

Mildew can be successfully removed from roses and pelargoniums by watering the plants occasionally with a mixture of one ounce of nitre dissolved in one gallon of water. An alternative remedy is to wash the diseased parts with a decoction of elder leaves.

Secrets for perfect flowers

Land that grows flowers to perfection, must be 'in good heart'. The experienced gardener must learn how much manure to add for each variety of flower.

The common nasturtium, if grown in highly manured soil, will produce an abundance of foilage but few blooms. If nasturtium seed be sown in rubbish, delightful flowers will be the result! But well-manured land is required for the raising of most quality blooms.

For very light soils, cow manure is the best substance to use. For a stiff cold clay, ashes from the bonfire, sand and strawy litter should be employed.

Slugs & Snails

Snails are particularly fond of bran moistened with vinegar. If a little is spread on the ground and covered over with a few cabbage leaves or tiles, they will congregate under them in great numbers. They can then be removed.

Another method

Place bran in a three inch pot which is laying on its side. The slugs will smell the bran and will happily eat it. The bran dries the slugs from the inside out and these make an attractive breakfast for small birds and hedgehogs.

Small Birds - To scare from Seeds

There are many ways of effecting this, but a clever mode of doing it is to stick a few potatoes over with white feathers and suspend them a few inches from the ground by means of a few threads of red worsted passed across your seed beds.

Snails and Worms

To prevent snails and worms crawling up trees, form a paste with train oil and soot and lay it on in a circle round the tree a few inches above the ground. This will form a barrier over which snails or worms will not pass.

Soot water

Soot contains a goodly proportion of nitrogen which is an invaluable fertilizer. It promotes good colouring with the aid of the carbon it contains. To make soot water, fill a bag with soot and suspend in a tub or bath of water for at least 24 hours, stirring from time to time. Even soot water requires to be diluted slightly before it is applied and as with all kinds of stimulants and fertilisers, care should be taken to guard against an overdose.

Stonework - To clean

Have the stone scrubbed with rain water, and when dry washed over with strong brine. This renders it white and sparkling, is no injury to the material, and it is a long time before any green stains appear, the brine being destructive to the germs of vegetation that adhere to the pores of the stone.

Tulips

Tulips, when cut early on a dull cold morning, are seldom very well expanded. If they are afterwards placed in a warm room and their stems put to stand in warm water, it will cause them to expand their flowers as well as they would have done on the brightest day in spring. This is not only applicable to tulips, but to many other flowers as well.

Turnips - prevent Turnip-Fly

This pest of the turnip crop is in reality a beetle, its scientific name being *Haltica nemorum*. Plenty of seed should be sown and damp weather should be chosen. Burning the surface of the soil and deep digging are beneficial as this tends to destroy the crysalids.

The most effectual banishment of the turnip-fly is secured by sowing the surface of the soil with gas lime two or three mornings after the seed is sown.

Varnish for Rustic Seats

One quart of boiled linseed oil and two ounces of asphaltum, to be boiled on a slow fire till the asphalt is dissolved, being kept stirred to prevent it boiling over. This gives a fine dark oak colour, is not sticky, and looks well for a year.

Or, first wash the furniture with soap and water and when dry, on a sunny day do it over with common boiled linseed oil. Leave that to dry a day or two, then varnish it over once or twice with hard varnish.

If well done this will last for years, and prevent annoyance from insects.

Vines

Bleeding in Vines

The usual practice of gardeners is to apply a hot iron to the bleeding surface until it is charred, and then rub into the charred surface a paste made of newly-burnt lime and grease. A more effectual application is thus made:-

One part of calcined oyster-shells beaten to fine powder in a mortar, and three parts of cheese, worked together, until they form a sort of paste. This mixture is to be forced into the pores of the wood, where bleeding takes place, by means of the thumb and finger. A second application is sometimes necessary.

Walnuts

Walnuts can be preserved with their shells clean. Allow the walnuts to stop on the trees till their outer husk begins to crack; then gather them, pick the husks off and lay them to dry. Then pack them in dry clean sawdust, enough to exclude the air from them. They should be kept in a dry room.

The sawdust from resinous woods should not be used.

Wasps' Nests - To destroy

Procure a glass bottle and rinse it out with spirits of turpentine. Thrust the neck of the bottle into the hole and stop it well round with mud, completely preventing the ingress and egress of the wasps. The fumes of the turpentine will soon destroy the wasps, so that the nests may be digged out a fortnight afterwards.

Waterproof Garments

To waterproof any sort of cloth or made garments all that is necessary is to make a very weak solution of glue or size (when cold it is weak and tremulous, about the consistency of calf's-foot jelly).

While hot, stir in a piece of alum till the taste of alum is distinctly perceived, when the piece is to be taken out. At the same time to add a little soap also, or rather soap-suds, to it, and then, while it is hot, to brush over the surface of the clothes with this solution.

Exposure to the air in the same way as sized paper is dried, completes the process of waterproofing.

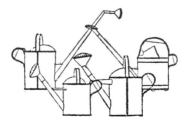

Withered Flowers - To revive

Plunge the stems of withered flowers into boiling water, and by the time the water is cold the flowers will revive. The ends of the stalks should then be cut off, and the flowers should be put to stand in cold water, and they will keep fresh for several days.

Worms - To drive out of pots

Securely cork up all the drainage holes in the pot, and then flood it for several hours with clear lime-water.

Please note:

Some of the traditional ingredients used in traditional recipes can be poisonous and although every effort has been made to avoid those ingredients it is recommended that you seek the advice of an expert before trying any new garden recipes.

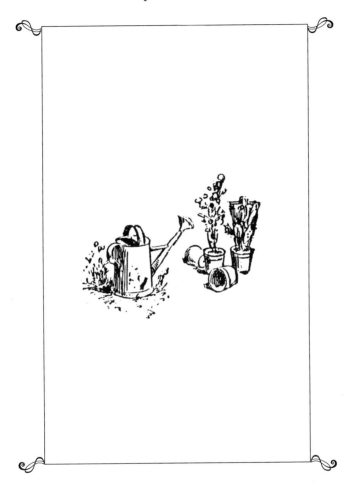

THE ETIQUETTE COLLECTION
Collect the set!
ETIQUETTE FOR COFFEE LOVERS
Fresh coffee - the best welcome in the world!
Enjoy the story of coffee drinking,
coffee etiquette and recipes.

ETIQUETTE FOR CHOCOLATE LOVERS
Temptation through the years.
A special treat for all Chocolate Lovers.

THE ETIQUETTE OF NAMING THE BABY
'A good name keeps its lustre in the dark.'
Old English Proverb

THE ETIQUETTE OF AN ENGLISH TEA
How to serve a perfect English afternoon tea;
traditions, superstitions, recipes and how to read your
fortune in the tea-leaves afterwards.

THE ETIQUETTE OF ENGLISH PUDDINGS
Traditional recipes for good old-fashioned
puddings - together with etiquette notes for serving.

ETIQUETTE FOR GENTLEMEN
*'If you have occasion to use your handkerchief
do so as noiselessly as possible.'*